First Published in paperback in 2015 by dinkylune

Second Edition Revised and Republished in paperback 2018 by dinkylune pty ltd

Copyright © 2018 by Kylie Dunn

Cover artwork created by Matthew Dunn (www.matthewdunnart.com)

Illustrations by Kylie Dunn

The moral right of the author has been asserted

All rights reserved

No part of this publication may be reproduced, stored in a retrieval system, or transmitted in any form or by any means, without the prior permission in writing of the publisher, nor be otherwise circulated in any form of binding or cover other than that in which it is published and without a similar condition including this condition being imposed on the subsequent purchaser.

The CIP catalogue for this title is available from the National Library of Australia

ISBN 978-0-9923583-6-5
ebook available from Amazon

Printed and bound in Australia by IngramSpark, Lightning Source Inc.

For Derek, without whom I would not have had the courage to take this on. Now can you just do the damn activity!

Thank you to my extremely talented brother, Matthew Dunn (matthewdunnart.com), for the front cover artwork and all the moral support.

Thank you to all my reviewers as well, especially Dana, Kat, Baden, Jo and Simon.

CONTENTS

What is all this about? 1
Background 4
    A note about purpose 5
The process 7
    The steps to my purpose 8
    A note on being kind to yourself 9
Step One – Watching the TED Talks 10
Step Two – Simon's website content 13
Step Three – Tony's personal strength reports 18
Step Four – Simon's book and Tony's audio 23
Step Five – Answering Tony's prompts 27
Step Six – Answering Simon's prompts 34
    Additional activity 41
Step Seven – Finding your values 42
Step Eight – Careers I've Considered 48
Step Nine – Drafting your purpose, belief and cause 52
Step Ten – Following your purpose 60
A bonus step – Defining success for yourself 67
    Intentional living 68
    A final note 74
Author Details 75
Connect with Me online 75
Other titles 76

WHAT IS ALL THIS ABOUT?

On the 1 November 2011 I started a year-long project to make some dramatic changes in my life. This project was called My Year of TED, since it was based around TED Talks from the popular TED.com website.

For those of you unfamiliar with TED, it stands for Technology, Entertainment, Design and is a wonderful "nonprofit devoted to Ideas Worth Spreading". They run a few conferences a year, and franchise a large number of TEDx events throughout the world. A large number of the talks from these events are available for free on their website ted.com.

There are a number of other activities and projects that they support, like the TED Prize and TED Ed, but you can find out about all of that on their website.

Why did I take on this slightly insane activity I hear you ask? I've been inspired by TED Talks for years and felt the urge to do something noteworthy and challenging to ring in my fortieth year on the planet. I felt that by 40 I should at least know who I am and what I wanted to achieve with my life, and I was certain that there had to be something in all of the wisdom of TED Talks to help me work that out – help me discover the authentic Kylie; what I wanted to give to the world; and to help me find my voice.

Inspiration struck when I watched Matt Cutts' talk, *Try something new for 30 days*. Something in this talk reminded me of A.J. Jacobs' *My Year of Living Biblically* — and the seed was sown. I decided to develop a list of activities based on TED Talks, and to try each one of them in my life for 30 days.

By the end of October 2012, I had completed twenty-one 30-day activities and one project — the development of the Do-Pad, a notepad for people who like to doodle, based on Sunni Brown's *Doodlers, unite!* I learned so much about my strengths, my weaknesses, my hopes, what I need in my life and, most of all, what I want to give this world. I am extremely proud that I finished the full year, and that I did it so openly and vulnerably.

You can read more about My Year of TED on my blog (www.kyliedunn.com) which has been captured in a book, *Do Share Inspire: The Year I Changed My Life Through TED Talks*.

LIVING WITH INTENT

The activities were emotional, particularly since they coincided with the stresses and demands of day-to-day life. Overall, here are the main lessons that I've taken away from this project.

- You never really know what you are capable of until you try. I'm stronger than I thought I was — certainly more so than I ever thought I could be.
- Being open about imperfections is important. It has deepened my connections with others.
- There is a power in simply doing something. Really, don't underestimate it.
- Sometimes you can be too introspective, to the point that it is not good for your mental health.
- If you are going to try something like this, you need to build in time to be kind to yourself.

In the end, I've developed a new appreciation for my capacity to be courageous. I've always known that I am a survivor, and I usually come out the other side of life challenges as a better person — if not a little more scarred and cynical. I always thought of strength and courage as qualities I wanted in my life but wasn't quite sure how to harness them. Now I see this is already inside of me. It's just one of the realisations this project allowed me to discover; which I continue to process.

30 days of Drive

This book is mainly based on Activity 6 from My Year of TED, which started in the middle of January 2012 and was called 30 days of Drive. It was designed around two TED Talks: *Simon Sinek: How great leaders inspire action* and *Tony Robbins asks why we do what we do*, with the objective of helping me define my Why and how I might achieve it.

Simon's talk presents the concept that great leaders and inspired organisations start from a point of Why and then move out to the How and What, and that this applies to individuals as well. Tony's presentation is about individual focus, target, belief system and fuel, and how these things define a person's drive.

In this book I will share the process I created for myself, so I could finally try to answer the question that had been plaguing me since childhood — what the hell do I want to do with my life?

The other bits

After the 30 days of Drive process I have included a bonus activity about success statements, which I created during Activity 16: 30 days of Choice. This activity, coupled with 30 days of Being Wrong, helped me realise I have had many instances in my life where I was too passive in the decision-making process.

Without knowing my purpose — without having an understanding of who I was and what I wanted to give the world — when I hit crossroads in my life I would often take the easiest or most comfortable choice. *I was not living an intentional life, because I was not intent on achieving any particular outcome.*

If you are anything like I was before I completed My Year of TED, then you are probably not living with intent either, so you know how painful and unfulfilling that can be. The activities in this book worked for me, if you have even half of the focus and determination I had, I know they will work for you too.

Links to other resources

There is a resource page on my website (www.kyliedunn.com/lwi-resources) which has some links that will be useful. You can also download a copy of a workbook to accompany this book, in case you don't want to complete the activities in the book itself.

LIVING WITH INTENT

BACKGROUND

This is not the first time I had tried to work out what drives me, or what my purpose is. This was something I had been thinking about on and off from high school. I was never lucky enough to be the kid who knew what I wanted to be when I grew up, or what I wanted for my future.

As a teenager, and a young adult, I always felt that not knowing what I wanted to do with my life was a massive failing. So many other people I knew seemed to have a purpose, or at the very least a path. The older I got the more I realised that there were few people who *really* knew – either they thought they knew; they were following a path that had been designed for them; or, they just thought that everyone else had it together and they didn't want to admit they didn't.

> UPDATE: Since completing my project another TED Talk has come along that shares the idea of multipotentialites (modern polymaths) — *Emilie Wapnick: Why some of us don't have one true calling*. The idea that a lot of people don't have a one thing would have changed my life when I was younger.
>
> I fully believe this is who I am — had I known about this idea at a younger age I wouldn't have felt like all my uncertainty and career changes were faults. Instead I would have known that they were part of my make up and a huge strength that would serve me well in future careers — and in achieving My Year of TED.

I knew some of the things I didn't want — I was never interested in being a mother and I was not interested in being ordinary. I also knew nothing I had done to date had hit the spot. It's not that I haven't enjoyed many of the roles I'd had in my career, it's just that I've always felt like something was missing. The easiest way to explain it is I've always felt like I should be doing something more; that I wasn't living up to my potential — as pompous as that sounds.

Even though this was something I'd thought about often in my life, I had never made a sustained and focused effort on trying to answer this question for myself. I think there was always a little part of me that was afraid to find out the answer to the question, because once you know you are required to do something about it.

There was another fear, and let's be frank about it, what if my Why was crap? What if after all my soul searching my Why was very mediocre?

I have a handful of books purchased at various times in my life I hoped would help me work things out, but that wasn't to be. The problem I found with the majority of them was they would tell you why it was important to know this stuff and what other people have done with the knowledge, they might have even hinted at how you could try to work it out, but none of them were practical. It is one thing I know about myself, I am a practical person. I'm happy to read the theory and get into the academics of things, but at the end of that I want a process dammit! I want you to give me some idea about how I might go about reaching the target.

That is the reason for the book, giving you some pointers so you can do something about it. It's not enough to treat this as an academic process that will satisfy the question, what I'm going to do is help you get to a point of knowing how to complete the outer layers of Simon Sinek's Golden Circle — the What and the How.

Remember, My Year of TED was all about the doing, and that is what this book is all about — what will you do when you know your Why? Developing this book is just one of many things I am doing to align what I do to my Why.

One last thing before we start, I won't guarantee that what worked for me will work for you. But I will guarantee that if you go through this process and do the work, you will know yourself better, and that's a great start.

A note about purpose

There is an article I discovered a week after completing the first version of this book. An interesting article by Kris Carr called *The myth of finding your purpose,* published on Huffington Post.

In the article, Kris explains that she does not believe that people's purpose should be an externally focused thing —

> *When our purpose is external, we may never find it. If we tie our purpose or meaning to our vocation, goal or an activity, we're more than likely setting ourselves up for suffering down the line.*

LIVING WITH INTENT

I won't write down here the words that went through my head, but I read on —

> *Your purpose is about discovering and nurturing who you truly are, to know and love yourself at the deepest level and to guide yourself back home when you lose your way. That's it. Everything else is your burning passion, your inspired mission, your job, your love-fueled hobby, etc. Those things are powerful and essential, but they're not your purpose. Your purpose is much bigger than that.*

And the thing is, I don't entirely disagree with her. I think what she describes so simply in the quote above is completely accurate, except that I would say there is a **P**urpose and a **p**urpose in our lives.

It should be everyone's **P**urpose to find out who they truly are; to nurture and love themselves; and be kind to themselves — at its most basic level this is what I wanted from My Year of TED. But there is a small 'p' **p**urpose as well, which is the way we talk about our why or drive; that thing we want to give to the world that will help us feel fulfilled.

This book is more about helping you find your **p**urpose, but along the way you will learn more about who you are and what you need from the world – so it will contribute to your **P**urpose as well. And that's the last word on that, I won't make any distinction about these concepts as we move through the Steps — promise.

THE PROCESS

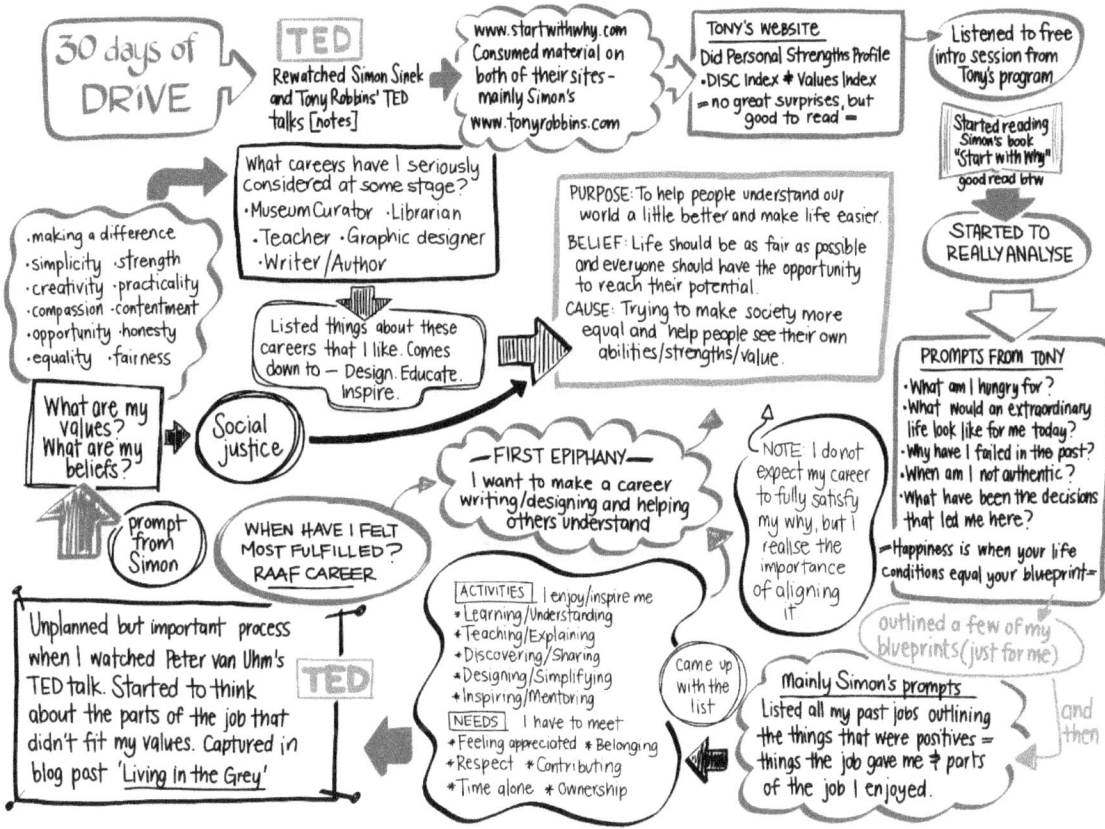

The graphic above is a revised visual representation of the 30 day activity completed as part of my reflection. It outlines the main steps in the process, and the outcomes of some of those steps — there's your process, thank you for your time.

Okay, so you're going to need a lot more than this graphic, or I hope you do otherwise I'll feel a bit dim given how much effort that process took me. I've broken the steps down into easy to follow instructions in this book, with the aim of helping you discover your purpose/why/drive, whatever you want to call it.

LIVING WITH INTENT

Somewhere in each of the ten steps in this book you will be prompted with questions to answer or activities to complete. This book also includes space for you to complete these activities or answer those prompts, or you can go to www.kyliedunn.com/lwi-resources and download a printable workbook.

The steps to my purpose

There were 10 steps involved in the process of trying to discover my purpose, some were more involved than others. The steps are:

Timing

Please remember that this was a 30 day activity for me, but I was dedicated to completing it within a set timeframe, so I was pushing quite hard at times. Some of these steps may take you days to feel like you have the right answers, so take the time that you need. It's important to finish, but it's more important to start doing something.

If you are inclined to lose focus or direction with these sorts of activities, then I would recommend setting an achievable deadline for yourself. Alternatively, you could put the pressure on someone else in your life to nag you about completing the process.

I am loathe to put a timeframe on it, because everyone is a little different and will be starting the process from a different point of self-awareness. I would say that if you have not completed the workbook after two months then you need to consider what your mental blocks are and how serious you are about the process in the first place.

Maybe it is an indication you are not ready to work this out yet, in which case I hope that you will come back to the book at a later stage and complete it. But if it is because you're unsure of the steps or what you might be trying to get out of them, I am serious about inviting you to email me. I will do what I can to help you through the problems, kylie@dinkylune.com.

> UPDATE: Alongside taking 30 days to initially complete this activity, I often return to the work and understanding from that time to update it. For most people, this is not static — remember the multipotentialites. So, feel free to make this iterative and realise you may not come up with definitive answers in this process. But you will certainly come up with a better direction.

A note on being kind to yourself

Just before we launch headlong into this process I would like you all to remember the final point in the things I learned from My Year of TED:

If you are going to try something like this, you need to build in time to be kind to yourself.

I cannot stress how important this is. If you are in a good place in your life, you might breeze this process. But if you aren't in a good place, if this does get confronting for you, and particularly if you are prone to negative self-thoughts (yeah, who isn't?) — make time to take a break and be kind to yourself.

I would recommend doing things like:

- going for a walk and being around nature, all the better if you have a pet
- being around people who make you happy and are very positive
- making something with your own two hands, it's a real self-esteem boost
- reading through My Year of TED blog, you'll feel better about yourself — I can almost guarantee it.

LIVING WITH INTENT

 # STEP ONE – WATCHING THE TED TALKS

This is as easy as the process gets, watch the TED Talks and answer a few questions.

I should start by saying there are a few TED Talks I could have selected as the basis of this activity, a lot of TED speakers discuss the importance of aligning your life and knowing yourself. The reason I chose Simon and Tony's talks is they are more practical than many of the others. This is sort of like the collection of books I have, they're interesting to read but have nothing meaty for practical application.

I had already watched both talks over a year before my TED project. I had actually watched Simon's a couple of times because I found it resonated with me as a concept. The way he defines the Golden Circle makes it so obvious that Why has to be the starting point for everything.

I had only ever watched Tony's talk once before because, well I find him a little annoying. I'm not saying that what he says is not valuable and important, I just find his style of motivational speaking is not for me. Maybe this has something to do with my introverted nature, and there is nothing wrong with that, but if you have the same reaction I would recommend pushing through.

I found that watching the talks again, with this activity in mind, gave me some new insights into the content of the presentations. Importantly, watching these talks again inspired me to believe that I could do this activity — maybe Tony Robbins was rubbing off on me after all.

Actions

* Watch *Simon Sinek: How great leaders inspire action* and *Tony Robbins asks why we do what we do*.
* Answer the following questions.

Is there anything about understanding your purpose you had not considered before listening to these talks?

___

___

___

___

___

___

___

Why is it important for you to do this activity?

___

___

___

___

___

LIVING WITH INTENT

What do you intend to do with the outcome?

_____

_____

_____

_____

_____

Each step along the way, I'd like you to be mindful about any internal pushback you might be experiencing. This could be as simple as thinking "oh I already know this" and trying to skip a step, or "I'll have to think about this" and then putting the book down to do something else.

While these thoughts might be true, they might also be blockages you need to address. Keep that in mind.

 # STEP TWO – SIMON'S WEBSITE CONTENT

I went through both Simon and Tony's websites to find any other material that might have provided some tips and guidance about this. The next couple of steps are based around that content, so I will summarise the basic ideas involved.

Simon Sinek's website, www.startwithwhy.com had a great Learning Library, with short conversations and articles to give more insight into his theories and what they mean in practice. I think I went through all the content during this step, but unfortunately this has been removed from the site, so I've provided a brief summary of the salient points.

My favourite podcast, I should mention they were only a few minutes long, was "How verbs help set measurable goals". I should admit that's mainly because I was working in government at the time and let's just say this is not something government does well. The most important podcast was "Course vs Cause", which I'm sad is longer available for you. It is such a simple yet powerful concept and could completely change the way you think about your life, so I've tried to give it some justice with the section below.

Below is my summary of the five podcasts that helped me develop a greater understanding of the ideas.

How verbs help set measurable goals – This is about setting values for organisations (which does translate to individuals). When you are setting values, you need to use verbs over nouns, because values are things you do (verbs); you can't do a noun.

Isn't this the most obvious statement in the world? But people do it all the time, there are so many organisations with Innovate and Honesty as values. Simon expands on this using the example of having "Do the right thing" not Honesty — not only is it actionable but it drives a higher standard.

> *Note: I should point out here that you might feel there is a contradiction to this later in the book. When we do the Defining your values activity you will be selecting them from a list that includes nouns. I don't think this is contradictory though because what you will be selecting are the important qualities for you, not defining actions you plan on taking.*

Identify your passion and take action – passion is not an actionable word, where does passion come from. It is a feeling you have when you are engaged in something you love, but Simon believes you should be that excited about everything you do in your life. What are the things you love to do and would do for free? You have to look deeper to find your passion in things — you need to think about what you enjoy, what you love and what they have in common.

Why is the start – finding your purpose is not the end of the journey it is the beginning of the journey. Your Why provides a marker to the kinds of things you should be giving your energy to that will bring fulfilment and greater happiness. Simon believes who we are is fully formed from the communities we grew up in, and that is set by about 18-19 years of age. Our Why comes from where we came from; the Why is the thing that drives/inspires you; and it comes from your past.

Simon's Why is to "Inspire people to do the things that inspire them". He feels happiest amongst those who are inspired to do things for others – around people who have the inner strength to help someone else find their own inner strength.

Happiness vs Fulfilment – this is the belief that we all have the right to live a fulfilled life from the work that we do. That everybody should love their job and be living a fulfilled life (I don't know that I fully agree with this, but more on that later). But this isn't the case, we are constantly looking for fulfilment. We're told money can't buy happiness but that is not true — money can buy happiness, but it cannot buy fulfilment. Happiness without fulfilment is a fleeting emotion, it is not sustainable. Someone who lives a fulfilled life has a sustained happiness that is always there.

Course vs Cause – this was the most powerful podcast, because I don't know that I would be capable of this. I am a planner and I love the certainty of a plan, but I completely understand the logic in what Simon says about this topic.

Simon explained that we feel we have to make plans even though nothing goes according to plan, and if we're obsessed with the plan we close our mind off to the other possibilities outside the plan. He explained that a plan is a course of action but — this is the epiphany bit — you need to focus on the **cause of action**, the destination. So many of our plans are focused on the route without knowing the destination. But how do you know you're going in the right direction if you don't know the destination? Of course, this is simple and obvious, isn't it?

If you do not know your destination, if you do not know your cause or your Why, then how do you know you are doing the right things in life? You may have a plan, but you are focused on the route because you don't really know where you want to end up.

Simon claims to be "agnostic about the route" since he has set the destination. That means, he is open to the possibility of options showing up, it is a longer term view.

Fulfilment without happiness

It is an interesting point that Simon makes about fulfilled people have a more lasting happiness. I've probably only had a truly fulfilling career once in my life and, looking back on it now, that fulfilment sustained me through a lot of crap. For three years of that career I was in a very destructive relationship; had to have neurosurgery; was overdosed on steroids, resulting in awful clinical depression; learned about some devastating things in the life of someone very close to me; confronted my parents about things that had happened in our childhood; lost my grandmother; and was completely betrayed by someone who supposedly loved me.

And yet, I still think of those years as being some of the most satisfying in my life — so maybe there is something in that. Or maybe it is a trick of the human brain that I've blocked out how painful and awful that period was, so I can think of it nostalgically? Nope, shame and humiliation are still there when I think of some of those things.

Actions

* Consider visiting Simon' website (www.startwithwhy.com) and see if any of the existing material is of interest to you.
* Answer the following questions.

LIVING WITH INTENT

Can you think of any times you have been fulfilled, not just happy?

LIVING WITH INTENT

Do you know anything about your destination, or have you just chosen a course? Where did you want that course to take you? Why?

 STEP THREE – TONY'S PERSONAL STRENGTH REPORTS

On Tony Robbins' website you can get a Personal Strength Profile (www.tonyrobbins.com/disc/). This is a DISC personality test that measures four dimensions of your behavioural style (Decisive, Interactive, Stability and Cautious), and provides you with a Values Index report, measuring your seven dimensions of motivation. These are available for free, if you give them your email address (which means emails about Tony's events), but I would recommend you take them to see if anything new comes up for you.

Note: DISC is a very popular personality test, so if you have already done this through your workplace or other course, you do not need to do it again.

Before I go through this, and before you take the tests, you need to remember they are time and place based. Personality tests do not tell you who you are, they simply collate the responses you give to a set of questions at this time and in this current mindset. Results can change, maybe not significantly but they can alter over time and after significant experiences or changes.

My Personal Strength Profile results were indicative of the Kylie that answered those questions in early January 2012. If I did this again today I think the responses in some areas would be quite different, but there is a lot that would stay exactly the same. So now I'm going to open the vulnerability gate a little wider and share my basic results with you.

The DISC Index goes through your natural and adaptive styles. Your natural style is how you behave when you are being authentic and true to yourself; making the adaptive style how you behave when you are aware of your behaviour or being observed. It's a comprehensive report, at 21 pages long, and has a lot of explanation about what the components and styles mean.

The majority of my results were not surprising.

- I was a deliberate and controlled problems solver (natural and adaptive).
- I was able to interact well but was more reflective than talkative (natural and adaptive).

- I was very conventional and liked having the whole picture before taking on a task (natural and adaptive).
- I was very calm, had a strong connection to my organisation, and was very patient with others (natural only).

This last point was the only semi-surprising result because my adaptive style was almost the complete opposite end of the spectrum, which values freedom of expression and the ability to quickly change focus. This might be one of the many reasons I found my working environment so stressful.

The report outlines topics of: ideas for being more effective; ideas for staying more motivated; strength-based insights for your behavioural style; ideal job/climate; areas for continual improvement; preferred training and learning style; communication insights for others (which in hindsight I should have printed and given to my boss at the time); and then has a series of questions for you to consider about your results.

The Values Index is more about your Why and finding your drivers. In my opinion these results are less likely to alter, being is more about your core values and passion. My Executive Summary looked like this:

High Aesthetic	You very much prefer form, harmony and balance. You are likely a strong advocate for green initiatives and protecting personal time and space.
Very Low Economic	You may try to help meet customers' needs (internal and external) before your own.
High Individualistic	You have no problem standing up for your own rights and may impart this energy into others as well.
Average Political	You are flexible, able to take or leave the power or clout that comes with the job title or assignment.
High Altruist	You have a high desire to help others learn, grow and develop.
Average Regulatory	You are able to balance and understand the need to have structure and order, but not paralysed without it.
Very High Theoretical	You are passionate about learning for its own sake. You are continually in learning mode and bringing a very high degree of technical or knowledge base credibility.

LIVING WITH INTENT

This is another very detailed report, 28 pages of analysis and then questions to make you think about how you can better align your environment with your passions. There are many things in just this table alone that explain why I had to leave my last job.

These were very interesting profiles about who I am and what I need to have in my environment to make me happy. Overall, I would have to say they are quite accurate, which is always a little scary.

These reports did inform some of the rest of the process, although I will admit I did not refer to them when I was pulling everything together. That is probably because they did not provide any earth-shattering insights about who I am, but they did validate what I thought I already knew about drivers.

> As an aside to this process, have you ever taken an Enneagram test? If not, I would recommend doing that one as well. It's a personality test which uses nine interconnected personality types which my boss at the time told me about. The types are: 1 Reformer; 2 Helper; 3 Achiever; 4 Individualist; 5 Investigator; 6 Loyalist; 7 Enthusiast; 8 Challenger; and 9 Peacemaker.
>
> According to the test, I'm an Investigator, which sat pretty well with how I thought of myself at the time. I should do it again, to see whether my post-MYoT type is the same.

No personality test can give you a definitive answer to who you are and what drives you, they usually capture your main preferences. This is particularly true of online tests that are generally a lot shorter, but I've always found them interesting — particularly the bits I don't agree with.

Actions

* Go to Tony's website and get your free Personal Strength Profile.
* Once you have the results, answer the following questions.

Were you surprised by the results in the Values Index? What don't you agree with? Ask someone who knows you well whether they see it differently to you.

LIVING WITH INTENT

Were you surprised by the results in the DISC Index? What don't you agree with? Ask someone who knows you well whether they see it differently to you.

STEP FOUR – SIMON'S BOOK AND TONY'S AUDIO

There were two parts of this step, the first was reading Simon Sinek's book *Start with Why*, which had some valuable prompts about the things I needed to start considering. Please note, it is not mandatory to purchase his book, his talk and the content on his website will provide you with enough of a grounding for the following steps. If you do wish to purchase it, or if your local library has a copy, it is an easy read.

The second part was listening to the free introductory session of Tony Robbins' *Ultimate Edge* program — again free means handing over your contact details. I found this very hard to get through, and since he apologises a couple of times for the length I mustn't be the only one. His presentation style is very draining, and it is two CDs worth of content — break it up into manageable chunks. There are some real gems in this once you get into it, so it's worthwhile pushing through.

Tony's course deals with a lot more than we're doing here, so there are a lot of valuable things that we won't discuss here.

If you don't have two hours of your life to dedicate to listening to Tony, or you don't think that you could do it without losing your mind, below are the ideas I found of most value from his introductory session.

"Wherever focus goes, energy flows" – you have to love a sound bite, and this is a pretty good one. It is true though, if you focus on negative things in your life or the things that could go wrong then you are putting all your energy into doubt and fear. My Year of TED taught me the value of focus, and the danger of it too.

This is important in relation to your drive because if you are focusing on achieving things that aren't part of your Why or don't sit with your values then you will have no energy for the things you want out of life.

Decisions shape destiny – this wasn't an epiphany, but he explains it well and did make me think about some of the decisions I have made that brought me to this point. This is something you will think about in the next step of the process. The general idea is that we have all made decisions to get to where we are, so we are all accountable for our life situation — put very simplistically. Following on from that thought, if you are responsible for creating it, then you are responsible for changing it.

The expansion of this is that even the simplest decision can have a major impact in your life. So, looking at this in relation to your purpose or Why, if you don't know what you want out of life or where you want to be then you are blindly making decisions that are shaping a destiny you are probably not going to be happy with. (This reminds me of Simon's Cause vs Course?)

Interestingly, in a later activity during My Year of TED I learned that it has been my lack of actively making decisions and just letting life take over, which caused the most grief for me in the past. Reflecting back on the failed marriages (yes, plural) I discovered that it was during periods of great uncertainty in my life that I just grabbed on to whatever option life threw my way. Unfortunately for me, during two of these times life threw me broken men I felt compelled to try to fix — that's a whole different book.

Why have I failed in the past? – the idea around this is the majority of people fail due to a lack of resourcefulness on their behalf. It's not that the goal was unobtainable it was simply that they didn't try hard enough, or they didn't use their resources well enough to succeed. This is a hard concept to think about because, as Tony explains, our resourcefulness is tied to our emotions. So, like the point above, we have nothing to blame but ourselves — and he's a motivational speaker? I guess knowing you are the one to blame is motivational, it gives you control but I think it also belies a whole heap of other influences that might actually be at play to create these issues.

Happiness is when your current life conditions equal your blueprint – this is so obvious, but I had a complete 'a-ha' moment about it (not the 80's pop band). The idea around this is we all have a story in our head about how the world should be, some blueprint about what life should look like. These blueprints are developed at a young age, and are usually someone else's blueprint, often our parents.

Even if you are successful in life, if what you're doing does not match your blueprint then you will not feel fulfilled. That means we have three choices:

- blame something else in our lives
- change our lives to match our blueprints
- change our blueprint to match our lives.

As you can imagine, blame is not the answer (dammit!). The best outcomes usually involve a mixture of change in life and blueprint.

Your blueprint is the idea you have of what you think you need to make you happy. The problem is we don't spend time in our lives actively designing these blueprints — humans are pretty bad at knowing what will make us happy.

Actions

In the next step we'll do some of the activities based on this introductory audio. For now:

- Listen to Tony's introductory audio or use the brief explanations above.
- Answer the following questions.

What were the most valuable parts of this content for you? Why do you think that is?

_____

_____

_____

_____

_____

_____

_____

LIVING WITH INTENT

Did you have any a-ha moments when you were reading? If so, make a note of them now as they might come in handy for future steps.

 STEP FIVE – ANSWERING TONY'S PROMPTS

There were a number of prompts in Tony's introductory audio, so I spent some time going through them to see what I might discover about myself. The first was defining my extraordinary life, which was interesting because there were only a few parts of this I could answer, which is why I was doing the activity in the first place.

It included things like living in the house we were building; not having to commute to work every day; being a successful, published author (that was one thing I knew I wanted); and being financially secure. Not all that extraordinary when you look at it like that.

Past failures were more confronting to consider at the time. This process paled into insignificance after I started 30 days of Choice and 30 days of Being Wrong, but that was six months after this process.

It's difficult to examine times you have failed; but it's even more difficult to think about it and consider how you could have avoided failure if you were more resourceful.

Actions

* Take some time to think about the following questions and record your answers below.
* Dig deep and be honest, you are the only one who will see this.

LIVING WITH INTENT

Answer: "What would an extraordinary life look like for me today?"

Why have I failed in the past? How was I not resourceful?

LIVING WITH INTENT

Decisions shape Destiny

This led to an exercise where I thought about some of the choices I had made that led me to where I was at the time of doing 30 days of Drive. It was an interesting exercise since some of my "bad" decisions were needed to get me to the place I was, which I was pretty happy with overall.

Of note would be my two failed marriages, that's right folks two of them. The interesting thing about them is without marriage number one I would not have ended up in Melbourne, which was a really important time in my life. I also may not have ended up joining the RAAF. I also met husband number two through friends I made during marriage number one, and without that relationship I probably would not have ended up pushing to be posted closer to Sydney. My career in RAAF Glenbrook was my most fulfilling role to date, and that was also where I met my wonderful partner Derek. So, even though they may have been poor decisions, they got me where I needed to be.

Okay, I was there without having to actually marry husband number two, but there were obviously a few lessons about myself that life decided I still needed to learn — the hard and tortuous way.

Actions

* Complete the activity below. You might be surprised what you come up with about what those decisions have ended up meaning in your life now.

List four decisions in your life you feel have had the greatest influence on where you are now.

Consider things like the decision you made on what to study, or when to leave school; a job or relationship you chose to take or leave; a decision to travel. It could be a really big decision, or it might have been something small at the time that has had a clear impact on your life.

What made you make the choice then, and how has it affected your life now?

LIVING WITH INTENT

LIVING WITH INTENT

Aligning current life conditions and blueprints

As outlined earlier, Tony talks achieving happiness when the reality of your life matches the design or worldview you have about it. I had never thought about it in this way before — what are the blueprints you hold now about your career, relationships or life in general.

It's fascinating to sit down and think about your blueprints, think about all the 'shoulds' you have in your worldview. There are a few of mine I was unaware of; some I addressed during My Year of TED.

There was one I will share with you, and it's probably the biggest one I had to tackle and find a way to rewrite. I didn't work it out during 30 days of Drive, I worked it out during 30 days of Time, but having the background from this experience helped me identify the problem.

During 30 days of time I realised my blueprint of who I am was based on who I was as a young teenager (probably about 14-15 years old). For some reason, whenever I thought about myself and my capacity to do things it was tainted by the sad, lonely, powerless and scared girl I was at that time. I had always wanted to be courageous, but I never saw that in myself — and this was the reason why, because my blueprint of myself did not match the reality of the strong, capable, courageous woman I had become.

I've spent a lot of time since then making sure I see the woman I am, and the woman I want to be. That girl is a part of me and she survived a lot to give me the life I have. Moving on from this blueprint means I have a much more positive view of myself and my past. Mainly, it's given me the ability to trust that I can do what I need to do to create the life I want.

Actions

* Complete the blueprints activity below. The focus is to find a blueprint you are unhappy with and work out how to change it. Start by thinking of an area of your life you are unhappy with, chances are this is a blueprint you need to understand and change.

Think about two blueprints, one you are happy with and one you are unhappy with; one part of your life that is aligned with your worldview and one that is not. In the boxes on the next page provide a brief explanation about the blueprint and what you like or don't like.

LIVING WITH INTENT

An area you are happy with – Why?

An area you are unhappy with – Why?

Consider the blueprint you don't like. Where does it comes from and what you would need to do to change it? Can you think of a new blueprint that would make you happier, that would give you a worldview closer to your current reality?

What is the blueprint you need to change?

 STEP SIX – ANSWERING SIMON'S PROMPTS

From Simon's prompts there were two exercises that helped me understand the activities that inspire and fulfil me, and the things I need from my environment. This was done by listing my favourite jobs, paying attention to the aspects of the job that worked for me — the bits I liked and the things they gave me.

The list below is the very simplified version I eventually came up with. I've just numbered them for simplicity rather than explaining what the job was and my job title.

1. Autonomy, no staff to manage, respect, creativity, mentoring.
2. Creativity, respect, peers, knowledgeable staff.
3. Peers, responsibility, ownership, felt like I achieved, challenges, money.
4. Autonomy, expert, made a difference, creativity, teaching, challenges.
5. Respect, expert, made a difference, creativity, teaching, learning, mentoring, belonging, autonomy, design, peers.
6. Respect, around smart people, autonomy, learning, design.

From this list, I picked the job that made me most fulfilled and expanded on the reasons why I think it was good for me. This was the Command Systems Information Manager role I did in the Air Force for about five years — the fulfilling career I mentioned earlier.

- I was the expert and generally well respected for my knowledge.
- I owned the whole thing and made the big decisions.
- I was able to teach, learn and come to an understanding of things.
- I had great peers to bounce things off, who were also good fun.
- I was able to do design work (documents, courses and web); teach myself new system functions and work out how it could support our needs; and develop a community of users across the country.

- I felt appreciated and valued by most of the people I engaged with.
- I felt like I was making a difference and leading a significant change process that would make things much better.
- I worked with minimal supervision, although one of my bosses did like to take all the credit.
- I was able to provide mentoring and support for four young troops, including helping them in their career decisions.

Below are the two lists I developed from these activities. I think they are important for me to include here as prompts for you, because I wasn't really sure what I was getting out of the activity for a while — hopefully they help.

Activities that inspire and fulfil me

Learning/Understanding – I love learning new things, which is probably why I love TED so much. I've always craved new information and knowledge in my life. But, while learning from experts is great, I probably enjoy learning through discovery more. When I'm able to work something out for myself and reach my own conclusions, that provides real fulfilment. This sort of thing doesn't happen in a vacuum — it involves reading and being exposed to a lot of intelligent people's ideas.

Teaching/Explaining – when I develop an understanding of something I get a certain amount of joy from it, but when I can explain that to someone else and teach them about it – that's a whole other level of fulfilment. For me there is no point learning if I'm just going to keep it all for myself, and as frustrating as explaining things to others can be, there is a distinct joy in the moment they understand it as well.

I should caveat this comment a little by saying I can be a knowledge hoarder at times. I enjoy being a *smart* person; I like people coming to me for answers and advice. But, to be brutally honest, I hate this about myself. It goes back to my struggle with self-esteem and reminds me how weak I still am.

Having said that, I'm good at explaining things to people, by this point in the book you may have your own opinion on that statement. There is also a little part of this that is about inspiring and mentoring. I get a real buzz from being able to help people in my life when they are trying to sort problems out and deal with issues in their lives. This surprises me to some degree, knowing some of my internal workings.

LIVING WITH INTENT

Discovering/Sharing – this is a little like the two points above, but I think of them as different things. I love discovering new things, and I particularly love it when I am the first in my social group to do so. This is why I enjoy StumbleUpon (and now Pinterest) so much. I have discovered so many things I would never have known about without a community of people providing links to it. When I discover particularly fantastic things, mind blowing ideas, cool music or art etc. I enjoy sharing it with people around me who I think would also love it.

Maybe this explains the librarian side of me, but I get a real buzz from being the person who has introduced someone to something new — it's a little like teaching/explaining. This also applies to discovering things about myself/human nature and sharing that with others. I have learned so much from people who are brave enough to share things about themselves, and I'd like to think that by sharing some of the things I learn about myself I might be helping someone else come to their own realisation.

Designing/Simplifying – from a young age I've always enjoyed being creative, drawing, painting and generally making things. In high school, I did graphic design for work experience, if I ever had something I thought I should be doing it was graphic design. But brick walls were put in my way, and in the words of Randy Pausch, I obviously didn't want it enough to push through the barriers.

Anyway, all of that aside, I have always enjoyed the parts of my jobs where I get to create. Designing and creating conference brochures, forms, documents, diagrams, training documents, websites and the like. I think this is what led me into information management, for me it is a very design related job, where the design is supposed to simplify the process of storing and locating information within an organisation.

This also leads me to have a lot of creative hobbies like jewellery making, card making and bookbinding. The most exciting thing for me now is that I am progressing a business concept where my creativity will be central to my daily activities. *Update: that did not progress, but I still hold out hope.*

Things I need from my environment

Writing this section on the blog was one of those very vulnerable experiences, it gave people the chance to understand how I work, and with that comes power. We all have triggers, things we need from the environment around us that make us happy. This section is a brief outline of some of the things I need to feel fulfilled in my environment.

Feeling appreciated – for me this is receiving acknowledgement and thanks for the things I do. This is, of course, a very common need in people. In particular, I need people to acknowledge things that have taken me a great deal of effort to do or are uniquely mine — yeah, I know that's not a clear definition, but I have never claimed I could clearly articulate all these thoughts and feelings.

Belonging – I didn't realise how much I crave this. I've always spent so much time in my own head and with my own thoughts, I didn't realise how much I need that sense of belonging. It's not like I need to be with people a lot, but I need to know I do belong to some sort of group of people. Realising this, I think I might finally understand my career in the Air Force — given I am not a military-oriented person that career choice was always a little odd for me. I think this the next need helps explain it too.

Contributing/making a difference – I need to feel like I am making a difference in the world; I am contributing to something significant. This is not unique to me, the majority of us need to feel like we are making a difference in some way. I should say that this "difference" can be done on an individual level, I just need to feel like I'm making a difference on some level.

Time alone – I am an introvert, so I need time alone to recharge my batteries and give my brain time to absorb and process the events of the day. This also translates into needing time alone during my work day to process and get my work done.

Ownership – I need to own the activities I am responsible for and have control over what I do and do not achieve. As you can see in the list above, autonomy features high on the scale for these positions, and one of the key requirements for autonomy is ownership.

Respect – I had left this out of the list when I initially created it on the blog, maybe because it is such a fundamental thing I didn't feel I needed to state it. I work hard to have the respect of people around me, and I need to respect the people I work for/with to enjoy my working environment.

Actions

✱ Complete all the activities below — you need to do this before Step Seven.

Remember these lists are just for you, so be as honest as you are brave enough to be.
There are no right or wrong answers here and you are not trying to impress anyone. The answers are based on your values and what makes you feel fulfilled or happy.

LIVING WITH INTENT

Pick your top five jobs or other roles you have had and write down some of the features, characteristics, or aspects that made you feel happy or fulfilled.

Job 1	

Job 2	

Job 3	

Job 4	

Job 5	

Are there any activities that appear regularly in the list above? Are there any similarities that give indicate what you are attracted to in a job? List them and write a brief define of that activity for you and why you think it is important.

Activity 1	
Activity 2	
Activity 3	
Activity 4	
Activity 5	

LIVING WITH INTENT

In the list of jobs, were there other values or characteristics that appear multiple times? Is there anything you can determine as a need you have from a job to find it fulfilling or enjoyable? List them down and why you think this might be important for you.

Need 1	
Need 2	
Need 3	
Need 4	
Need 5	
Need 6	

The lists you have come up with here are an important part of the following step on values, so **please make sure you have completed this step before moving on.**

Additional activity

I've thought about this quite a bit since first publishing the book. I don't believe that *follow your passion* is great advice for anyone. But I do believe that understanding your passion can help you identify your Why.

Why is it crap advice? I've always had two issues with it; not every passion can become a profitable career and commoditising your passion is problematic.

For example, you might love oil painting and have a burning passion for creating beautiful pieces for friends and family. But, not many people would be able to live entirely off the average income from an oil painting career. Furthermore, becoming a professional painter means becoming a marketer, salesperson, administrative person, accountant etc. unless you can start out with enough money to hire all these people — if you do then you are also a manager now.

I prefer to think of it as understanding your passion and understanding how you might choose a career that either aligns to that or doesn't interfere with that.

So, our oil painter might choose to be an art teacher for alignment, or they might choose a job that doesn't require a lot of energy, so they can use their evenings and weekends to create.

What are you passionate about? Think about your passions and what it is about that activity that you really enjoy — our oil painter might say creating and playing with colours.

LIVING WITH INTENT

 # STEP SEVEN – FINDING YOUR VALUES

This step comes from Simon Sinek again, it is about identifying your values and beliefs, because they are an integral part of your Why. This was another challenging activity for me, as another TED Talk was put online that made me question how much I compromised my values when I was a member of the RAAF. There is a whole blog post on www.kyliedunn.com about this called *Living in the Grey* that will explain the issues in more detail if you are interested.

I don't think I ever realised how important it is to ensure what you do aligns to your values, or at the very least does not conflict with them. I know this is obvious, but it is amazing how many things you may know intellectually and yet you don't ensure you are operating that way.

> *This was one of the key lessons for me from My Year of TED, stop making all these things intellectual pursuits and start making them practical.*

After I understood my values I could see the main reason I had left pretty much every job, and why I was unhappy in the organisation I was working for. It explained the two failed marriages as well, but I think you've heard enough about them. Most importantly, once you know these things you must do something about it, or you'll increase your pain.

To assist in this exercise, I searched the web for a list of values I could use, rather than trying to think about values that were important to me. There is always the danger you will forget something important — like respect from the list of needs for instance. The list I found was not perfect, there are some values on there that I don't even think are real words, but it was a great start. Since that time, I have redeveloped the list from multiple other sources, and my own growing appreciation of the topic.

The three step process below has evolved from other sources, and my experience. I managed to get my list down to the 12 most important values, although there were only 11 originally published. I had removed Intelligence from the list published on the blog because — to be quite frank — I wasn't brave enough to include it. So, the unabridged list from 2012 is:

LIVING WITH INTENT

- Making a difference
- Simplicity
- Strength
- Creativity
- Practicality
- Compassion
- Contentment
- Opportunity
- Honesty
- Equality
- Fairness
- Intelligence

What I realised from this process was, I have a very strong drive for social justice in my values. I have a strongly held belief that people should be treated fairly and equally; *__none of us is any better than anyone else simply by the vagaries of birth, privilege, education or position.__* Most importantly, we should all be given the opportunity and encouragement to reach our potential, whatever that may be.

I will add, I am not some idealist Pollyanna about this, it is the ideal I work towards. I realise there are many reasons within a person that might stop them achieving their full potential, even with all the support and opportunity in the world. But we are all entitled to a chance to reach our potential, not just accept our lot in life.

Determining your personal values

I have adapted this exercise from the Mind Tools website and Simon Sinek's prompts. It's an activity I include in my free workbook *Living with Intent*, and I've led people of varying ages through it successfully.

Actions

There are three tasks in this step which look very simple in a list like this, but you might find it difficult limiting your list to ten:

1. Time and place – try to think of what values make you feel happy and/or fulfilled based on previous experiences, Step Six will assist with this.
2. Selecting your top ten – select your ten core values from the list provided.
3. Prioritising your values – prioritise your top ten values.

LIVING WITH INTENT

Task 1 – Time and place

The idea of this is to try to think of what values make you feel happy and/or fulfilled. From Step Six you should have a pretty clear indication of these, but they were work related activities. For this activity I want you to think of three times in your life you were happy, proud or fulfilled — personal or professional. What were you doing? Who were you with? What do you think contributed to these feelings?

In brief summary, my three times were:

- my RAAF career, of course, which included purpose, belonging, contributing and feeling valued
- the year after I left my first husband, because I set three goals and achieved them – skydiving, going to Italy and joining the RAAF
- any time in my life I'm creating, it gives me freedom, pride and a sense of achievement.

Use the boxes below to flesh these out a little and try to capture the essence of what those feelings were.

The next page is a list of personal values. I'm sure it is not definitive, so if there is something not on this list feel free to include it in your values anyway.

Acceptance	Contribution	Friendliness	Love	Security
Accountability	Control	Friendship	Loyalty	Self-control
Achievement	Courage	Frugality	Making a difference	Selflessness
Adaptability	Creativity	Fun	Mastery	Self-reliance
Adventure	Credibility	Generosity	Maturity	Self-respect
Affluence	Curiosity	Goodness	Meaning	Serenity
Altruism	Daring	Grace	Mindfulness	Service
Ambition	Decisiveness	Gratitude	Modesty	Significance
Appreciation	Dependability	Growth	Morality	Silliness
Approachability	Desire	Happiness	Neatness	Simplicity
Assertiveness	Determination	Hard Work	Open-mindedness	Sincerity
Awareness	Devoutness	Harmony	Openness	Sophistication
Balance	Diligence	Health	Optimism	Spirituality
Beauty	Discipline	Heart	Order	Spontaneity
Being the best	Discretion	Helping society	Originality	Stability
Belonging	Duty	Honesty	Passion	Strength
Boldness	Dynamism	Honour	Peace	Success
Bravery	Ease	Hopefulness	Perceptiveness	Thankfulness
Calmness	Effectiveness	Humility	Perfection	Thoroughness
Capability	Efficiency	Humour	Perseverance	Thoughtfulness
Care	Elegance	Imagination	Positivity	Traditionalism
Certainty	Empathy	Impact	Power	Trustworthiness
Challenge	Enthusiasm	Independence	Practicality	Truth
Cheerfulness	Equality	Inner harmony	Pragmatism	Understanding
Clarity	Excellence	Inquisitiveness	Pride	Uniqueness
Collaboration	Excitement	Insightfulness	Privacy	Unity
Commitment	Experience	Integrity	Professionalism	Usefulness
Community	Expertise	Intelligence	Prosperity	Virtuous
Compassion	Exploration	Intimacy	Purposeful	Vision
Competence	Fairness	Introspection	Quality	Vitality
Competitiveness	Faith	Intuition	Realism	Warmth
Composure	Family	Joy	Refinement	Wealth
Concern	Fidelity	Justice	Reliability	Willingness
Confidence	Fitness	Kindness	Resilience	Wisdom
Connection	Flexibility	Knowledge	Resourcefulness	Wittiness
Consistency	Focus	Learning	Respect	Wonder
Contentment	Freedom	Logic	Restraint	Youthfulness

LIVING WITH INTENT

Task 2 – Select your top 10

From the list on the previous page, select the ten values you feel best describe who you are and what is most important for you — remember honesty.

I went through the list three times before I managed to get it down to 12 core values, so I have included a couple of extra spots. The important thing to remember is these are your top ten values, there will be other values in the list that are important to you at different times, but you're trying to find the core values that define and inspire you.

Task 3 – Prioritise your values

Do any of the values you have selected contradict each other? Are any in direct conflict with each other? If so, which one takes priority?

In this section you need to work out the order in which you would satisfy them, if you had to make a choice. For example, if you have Generosity and Stability on your list and a friend needed to borrow $100, which is all you have in the bank until pay day next week, which value would take priority?

Below, write down the prioritised order of your values, so you now have a list of 10 prioritised values — drop any extras you might have had form the previous task. You may find you will go back and make some adjustments to this list in the next couple of weeks or months, as this all sinks in you will develop a greater appreciation of yourself and your values.

It is also important to remember this is still a time and place activity. While your core values won't change dramatically in your life, their importance at any time might change. So, since I've had you narrow it down to ten you might find the couple you rejected might move up and onto the list.

You may also have something occur in your life that brings something new onto the list. Don't be afraid to revisit this, it should reflect who you are, not who you were, if it is to be a valuable resource for understanding yourself and your purpose.

1.	6.
2.	7.
3.	8.
4.	9.
5.	10.

 # STEP EIGHT – CAREERS I'VE CONSIDERED

The last list I developed was a list of the careers I have thought about pursuing at some stage. I know I've said I didn't know what I wanted to be when I grew up, but that doesn't mean I hadn't seriously considered career options.

The careers that have come back several times, some of which I've done some study in, were:

- Museum curator – I probably would have accepted working in a museum just researching the collection. I love the concept of this, working in a quiet place with collections that need to be classified and researched. Which is probably why another of the professions I've considered is…
- Librarian – this started at a young age because I loved the library. It was a quiet place where you were surrounded by books, what's not to love? Interestingly, I do have a librarian qualification, my Information Management graduate diploma is a recognised qualification in Australia. I also had an organisational library as part of my responsibilities in a previous role, so I have been able to play in this space a little.
- Teacher – I don't know how many times I have seriously entertained the concept of teaching, probably too many to have never done it.
- Graphic Designer – I've mentioned this one earlier as the career I should have pursued after school. Given all the things I do as a hobby and how much I enjoy doing any sort of design work in my jobs, I think I would have enjoyed this option.
- Writer – copywriter, technical writer or any sort of writer — author was the dream. When I look at it I've spent so much time writing throughout my public service career that I have been a writer in many ways. The problem was I always had someone telling me what to write and the style to write it in. That would continue to be a problem if I did it as a career — unless I do it this way I guess.

After analysing the bits of these careers that appeal to me I came up with three words — Design, Educate, Inspire. This might appear to ignore the museum and library roles, but I guess that's how you see those jobs. For me they are education focused roles, where you are providing well designed and inspiring environments to stimulate the learning process.

Another interesting way to look at these careers is most of them fairly quiet careers, which would require a lot of alone work — and then there's teaching. This would probably be a good indication of why I have never pursued it as a career option, I just don't know how I would survive in that environment on a daily basis. I could also add, people seem to think I am a lot more patient than I feel I am, so I don't know whether I could not lose it with students.

> UPDATE: Since leaving my government career, I spent a bit of time trying to work out what I could do to achieve my Why. Interestingly, I now spend a lot of time facilitating business training — including qualifications — for a living. It's a role that caters to that need to help other people learn, while not putting me in a classroom with teenagers. I'm not entirely sure it's a 'forever' type role for me, but I'm enjoying the challenge and changes.

Careers you've considered

You need to step completely out of reality for this one. By that I mean don't consider whether you *could successfully* step into this career — this isn't about picking a job it is about identifying the sort of things you would love to do and why.

Once you have outlined all the careers the idea is to see if there are any themes you can identify about these careers. Consider all the facets of the careers, because the themes may not be very obvious at first.

Actions

* Identify five careers you have considered, pursued or are currently doing. If there are more than five, grab another sheet of paper.
* Examine aspects and identify any themes.

LIVING WITH INTENT

Capture titles and most appealing aspects of the job for you. Consider environment, challenges, stature, dynamics, money, benefit, etc. Try to think of what it represents rather than what it is.

Job 1	
Job 2	
Job 3	
Job 4	
Job 5	

From this list can you identify any themes? These could be things like 'helping others', 'being in charge', 'security', 'freedom', etc. This is based on how you see these careers.

STEP NINE – DRAFTING YOUR PURPOSE, BELIEF AND CAUSE

By this stage you should have a book full of lists, a clearer idea of your values, and a stronger idea of what drives you. If you don't have these things then you're probably not ready for Step Nine, because this is where you try to pull it all together to come up with some definitions.

My process was to sit down with everything I had done and try to draft a Purpose, Belief and Cause — which combine to be my Why. I drafted these definitions knowing they would be an evolving thing, since it's not easy to put language around something that is so intrinsically you. Simon talks about this a lot in his work, the fact that your Why lives in your limbic brain, which has no access to the language centre of your brain. It's a theory that helps explain why we find this stuff so difficult to pin down.

One of the things I had done was write down a few statements during the process, about things I enjoyed doing or things I had realised I believed in life.

- I want to make a career writing, designing and helping others to understand their world.
- I want to create simple, practical, elegant and easy to understand resources to aid this purpose.
- It is important to me that people are not discriminated against in any capacity, whether that discrimination is intentional or not.
- It is important to me that everyone has the opportunity to reach their potential, especially as children.
- It is important to me that, as much as possible, life is fair.

Actions

* Take a few minutes now to write out five statements of things you might want to do, things you believe are important, and things you think may drive you.

LIVING WITH INTENT

1.

2.

3.

4.

5.

LIVING WITH INTENT

My definitions

When I was drafting the definitions, I started with my Cause, which I had worked out has a very strong social justice bent to it from my values. This made my Belief pretty obvious, so that took no time at all to define.

My Purpose took a little longer, and whilst I'm comfortable with the intent of it, the language still needs some work.

> **Purpose** – *To help people understand our world a little better and make life easier.*
>
> **Belief** – *Life should be as fair as possible and everyone should have the opportunity to reach their potential.*
>
> **Cause** – *Trying to make society more equal and help people see their own abilities/strengths/value.*

These definitions have continued to go through some tweaks and changes, but they maintain the same general meaning.

Please remember, for me this was part of a broader project where I had already spent three months being introspective and aware of my thoughts and feelings. I don't know whether this would have worked as well without the project, especially since the project itself, and sharing through the blog, had given me some great insights into my drive.

I had also done a mini process about my focus and priorities for 2012 to develop my three words (Do. Share. Inspire.). This also helped with this process.

By the way, the three words is an idea from Chris Brogan. Instead of a New Year's resolution you select three words that will define what you want to focus on or achieve in the following 12 months. I've done this every year since My Year of TED – you can search for the posts and reflections on my blog.

Drafting your statements

Now it's your turn to complete the final step of drafting your Purpose, Cause and Belief. We're going to start with a bit of brainstorming, then move into writing the final statements.

I'm a keen visual note taker, so part of this activity involved creating a mindmap of the words and concepts around these three elements, to see if a statement would leap out at me — or at least hop out a little.

For those of you who have not done a mindmap before, the basic idea is that you put the subject in the centre. You then create a visual network on the words, ideas and concepts that are related to that central subject, using interlinking lines to show the relationships. For more information try Wikipedia's definition or search Google images for mindmap and you will get some fantastic examples.

The real value of capturing your ideas in this way is that it frees your brain from linear thinking. By putting words randomly on the page, you are more likely to see the connections. It doesn't work for everyone but give it a try.

I would recommend grabbing a large sheet of paper to do this, but I have included space if you want to do it here in the book.

Actions

* Read through the prompts for each of the words and brainstorm the ideas, phrases or words that you feel define this for you into a mindmap.
* If a statement leaps out at you, then capture it on page 59, otherwise move to the next concept.

LIVING WITH INTENT

Let's start with your Cause

- The definition of a cause is "A person or thing that gives rise to an action, phenomenon, or condition".
- If you look at my statement for Cause it can be summed up in one word — equality.
- When you look at your values, the things that have been important to you in the past, the things that have made you happy or fulfilled, what words define what has driven you? Was there an underlying motive behind the decisions that you made? Remember, be honest about this, no one is judging you here.

CAUSE

Move onto Belief

- The definition of belief is "Something one accepts as true or real; a firmly held opinion or conviction".
- At the very core, my Belief is that life should be fair — I know it's a pipe dream.
- From all the information you have gathered, can you define your deepest held conviction about the world? This should tie in closely with your Cause, so keep those words in mind when you're defining your Belief. Pay particular attention to your blueprints and values.

BELIEF

LIVING WITH INTENT

Lastly, onto Purpose

- The definition of purpose is "The reason for which something is done or created or for which something exists".
- When I went through this process the thing that kept coming up for me was helping people understand, the rest is just padding.
- Go back through everything you have so far, look at your Cause and Belief and ask yourself "Is there any underlying aim or intent in the things I have done in my life?" I found the Careers you've considered from Step Eight a great prompt for this definition.

PURPOSE

There is no shortcut to this process and there's not a lot of additional guidance to give other than keep going until you feel comfortable with the words you are using. If it doesn't feel right go and look at a thesaurus and see whether there are other words that fit better.

I sat with mine and tweaked them for about five days before I put them online, and they have continued to evolve a little since then. It might help to write them up and stick them somewhere obvious, so you are forced to live with them and think about them every day.

The last thing I will suggest is coming up with some scenarios to test them. This might be reliving a big decision you have made in your life and looking at whether your definitions played a part in that process. Or by thinking about a decision you might have to make, or even want to make — a dream job scenario or a relationship.

After you have lived with these concepts for a couple of weeks, and made adjustments until you are happy with them, you need to put the rest of the words in to make the statements — if you haven't already.

Actions

✱ Finalise the three statements – for now at least.

Cause

Belief

Purpose

LIVING WITH INTENT

 # STEP TEN – FOLLOWING YOUR PURPOSE

Defining your Why

When I came up with the three definitions above they felt right, even though the language of my Purpose is a little clunky. From Simon's work, the important part of this definition is your belief. Go back and look at it again. Is that who you are? Is that the basis of your decision making and how you live your life? Because in the now you're going to try to work out how to follow it.

I've mentioned a few times in this process how important it is to ensure your life is aligned to your Purpose – this includes your Belief, Cause and the values you defined in Step Seven. If you are living a life that is out of sync with these things you may feel unsettled, frustrated, depressed and angry — you will definitely feel unhappy and unfulfilled.

I had never articulated these facets of my life before, and although I knew things like fairness, equity and opportunity were important to me, I wasn't consciously aware of how important they were. Even though I may not have known consciously, I can see now I've been most unhappy when I've been doing things that were not aligned with these definitions. More importantly, I've felt fulfilled when I've been doing things that are aligned.

An example of the frustration of misalignment was in my RAAF career. I had a few years where I didn't have to face a lot of sexism, not in my day-to-day team environment anyway. When we had a handful of new people posted in that changed, rapidly and radically. It started with questioning my judgement on things and ended up with being completely marginalised from the training and support process, which I had developed and run for the previous two years.

When they were marginalising the female troops as well, giving them the crap jobs while the male troops got the fun trips with the officers, it all started to get too much. I tried to bring the matter up but didn't make any ground — I was being too sensitive, or I was reading the situation the wrong way.

I spent my last year in the RAAF being very angry at what was happening, and the inequity of the treatment and respect people were shown. Maybe I should have done more, but there was a culture I wasn't strong enough to fight against. So, when my short service commission ended I refused to stay in uniform any longer, for which I also received criticism.

I've had a few other experiences like this, none as lengthy or extreme as the RAAF. Once I completed this process I understood my level of frustration and dissatisfaction in more detail. It helped me understand why I was unhappy with some of my jobs, especially when they seemed so good on paper.

So, what now?

Going back to Simon Sinek's work, once you know your Why you can start to develop your How and What. In Simon's terminology:

- the Why is your Belief or your reason for doing what you do
- the How is the action you take to realise that belief, it is based around your values (so we're already primed for that one)
- the What is the result of the action (or the How).

So, my underlying belief is that life should be fair, and that people should be given equal opportunity to reach their full potential. (WHY)

I try to achieve this by helping people move towards their potential, helping them realise and understand opportunities, and inspiring them to take action. (HOW)

My blog, books like this, developing resources that help people learn about themselves and achieve fulfilment. (WHAT) This is the crux of my business, and the facilitation I've been doing.

For many people life does not provide a lot of opportunity to be able to fully realise the What that would satisfy your Why, so you may have to be pragmatic about it. But for now, let's imagine a perfect world.

Actions

* Answer the following questions "in a perfect world" scenario; not taking into account limitations on money, time, locations or skills.

LIVING WITH INTENT

Is there something you have in your life now that fulfils your purpose? If so, explain what it is and whether you believe it is enough?

Based on your purpose, belief, cause and values, what actions do you think would best satisfy your belief (remember in Simon's language this is your Why)?

What would be the result of these actions?

LIVING WITH INTENT

Define a draft Why, How, and What at this stage?

My draft Why
(this is basically your Belief from earlier, you need to connect with it emotionally)

My draft How
(the action/s you do to realise your Why, can take the form of value statements)

My draft What
(this is the marketable result of that action, how you explain what you do to others)

Do you currently live the actions of your How? Are you able to deliver your What to the world? If not, what is stopping you from doing these things?

What do you have to change to make them achievable?

LIVING WITH INTENT

Are you willing to make these changes? If not, what are you willing to change?

 # A BONUS STEP – DEFINING SUCCESS FOR YOURSELF

I realised there was an exercise from another activity in My Year of TED that would be very beneficial for you in this process. During 30 days of Choice, I used Alain de Botton's TED Talk, *A kinder, gentler philosophy of success*, as the basis for an exercise to develop "success statements" for myself. They are aimed at reducing envy and the desire to compare yourself with other people.

As Alain explains, we tend to compare ourselves to people who we feel are like us, since we could envisage ourselves having what they have. His concept of success statements is that by knowing what success would look like for you, in all aspects of your life, you are less likely to be envious of people who achieve things you actually don't want for yourself anyway. As well as that, the statements will reduce your envy of people who achieve something you want, but at the expense of something that is very important to your overall definitions of success – career over a relationship, or financial stability over health.

The statements will assist you in two other areas as well:

- Decision making – since they define your goals in each major area of your life it is easier for you to ensure your decisions are moving you towards your goals. They are particularly powerful in helping you evaluate the pros and cons of unexpected opportunities.
- Identifying unhelpful blueprints – in Step Four I asked you to identify a blueprint that was not very helpful for you. When you are defining success statements it is a perfect opportunity to see if there are any ideas that are in conflict with each other. For example, your Family statement might include being home for dinner every night with your spouse and kids, but your Career statement is to be the CEO of a multi-national corporation — these two things cannot co-exist.

Visit the resource page on the website to watch a brief video about this idea.

LIVING WITH INTENT

Intentional living

All the exercises you have completed so far are helping you create a life of intention, rather than the passive life many people tend to live. These statements are probably the greatest contribution to that intent, since they allow you to understand what you want from your life, and what you want your life to look like.

Once you have that understanding, and you combine that with all the work you've completed on your Why, What and How, it will change the way you think about what you are doing and the opportunities you want to create for yourself.

Categories for success

During the activity, I identified ten areas of my life I felt should have success statements — Relationship, Friendships, Family, Finance, Career, Learning, Hobbies, Volunteering, Mental health, and Physical health. You might have other important areas of your life that would also benefit from a success statement — maybe travel, or parenting. I've included some additional space for you to define them.

Success statements need to be written as a situation that *is*, rather than something that ***will be***, so "I am" and "I have" statements. When I first wrote my statements, I knew they would be going on the blog, so they were not as detailed as they could be. But those have also had some minor adjustments in the last few months, and are now a little more detailed:

Relationship – I am in a happy, loving relationship with someone who loves me and supports me in everything I do. He is also willing and able to take care of me when I can't take care of myself.

Friendships – I have a small number of people in my life who are positive and supportive, who I can rely upon and who can rely upon me. These are people I can be myself around without fear of judgement, and people who are also interested in improving themselves and the world around us.

Family – I have mature, supportive and non-destructive relationships with all my family members and I am a wonderful aunt to all of my nephews and nieces. I have reasonable expectations of who they are and what our relationship will be.

Finance – We own our own home and have the money to maintain it easily. I am able to afford to live a comfortable lifestyle where I don't have to think too much about money, meaning I can generally do what I want without too much restriction — importantly this means we travel to visit family and friends as and when we want.

Career – I have a career where I am respected, valued and contributing to society. I have established a business for myself that is successful, fun and aligned to my Why. I am a published author with regular speaking engagements, who is inspirational and influential.

Learning – I am continuing to learn in formal and informal ways; sharing those learnings with others. Learning is not a purely intellectual exercise for me, I put those learnings into practice in my life.

Hobbies – I have creative outlets in my life that allow me to express myself and make beautiful objects that are appreciated by others. I ensure I have time to pursue them in my busy schedule.

Volunteering – I am engaged in a volunteer role that allows me to give back to my community in a meaningful way.

Mental Health – I am happy, a lot nicer to myself and experience very few melancholic or blue moods. I no longer experience any periods of clinical depression.

Physical Health – I am physically healthy and have more positive control over my weight and the ongoing health issues I have to manage.

Actions

* Write a sentence or two for each topic that describes what success looks like for you. They must be written in the terms of having achieved the success — so "I have…" and "I am…", not "I will…" or "I want…" — and should be very descriptive.

Remember this is about what success in these areas would look like for you — not your parents, friends, teachers, partner etc. — be honest and true to yourself.

LIVING WITH INTENT

Relationship:

Friendships:

Family:

Finance:

LIVING WITH INTENT

Career:

Learning:

Hobbies:

Volunteering:

LIVING WITH INTENT

Mental Health:

Physical Health:

WHERE TO FROM HERE?

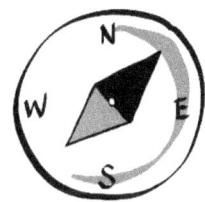

It is important to remember you don't need to have everything perfectly aligned in your life to be following your purpose or satisfying your Why. For those of you who have a mortgage and a family it might not be possible to ditch the high paying career to pursue your Why. So, let's take the pragmatic approach about what this all means and what you will do as you plan your next steps.

1. Few things are completely perfect in life, but you need to ensure the important things (career and relationships) are not in conflict with your values and your beliefs.
2. Volunteering opportunities can often fill a gap if you are not able to change your career or job. Consider whether there is a volunteering opportunity that aligns with your purpose and make the time to include it in your life.
3. Hobbies can also provide a great deal of satisfaction around your Why, depending on what it is of course.
4. Take small steps towards what you think you might want to achieve, you might work out that it all looked good on paper but the How and What you imagined are not going to give you what you needed.
5. Find supportive people around you and let them know what you want out of life and how you think you want to achieve it. You never know what opportunities will come up when you share with others — be brave

Remember, this will continually evolve as you move through your life and things change for you. Consider how you will revisit these ideas, particularly your success statements. Don't think of this as a set and forget activity, try to use it to inform your decisions and make changes if/when it isn't working for you any longer.

A final note

I hope that you have been able to get what you wanted out of the book. Thank you for giving me the time to share my insights with you and help you through what I believe is a daunting process. The important thing to walk away from all of this with is a better understanding of who you are and what you need from the world. These things will help you start developing intention in your life, which will lead to greater fulfilment.

I would love to know how this went for you, so please feel free to leave a comment on the My Year of TED Facebook page or send me an email kylie@dinkylune.com. Feedback is always appreciated, and I am happy to provide any additional advice and guidance, if I can, as well.

Please also consider giving the book a review on Amazon, so other people will have a better idea of what they might get from this book.

Kylie.

AUTHOR DETAILS

On 1 November 2011 I embarked on a crazy project I had created for myself called My Year of TED, to attempt to find my authentic self. Using the wisdom of world-famous TED Talks, I set about completing twenty-one 30 day activities, blogging about the whole adventure at www.kyliedunn.com. I've made significant changes through the project, and now I'm trying to share with others through a series of books and practical guides.

CONNECT WITH ME ONLINE

You can also connect with me online to stay up to date and ask me question. I'm always happy to discuss my work and give you pointers on the processes I suggest:

Twitter: www.twitter.com/dinkylune

My Year of TED blog: www.kyliedunn.com

Facebook: www.facebook.com/MyYearofTED/

OTHER TITLES

- *Do Share Inspire: The Year I Changed My Life Through TED Talks* — read the blog of My Year of TED in book form.
- *Write to Launch: A Step-by-Step Guide to Self-Publishing* — if you want to do this for yourself.

I continue to write further books and content around My Year of TED activities. I also create a range of free resources for my subscriber community to provide understanding yourself and creating the life you want.

You can sign up to my subscriber community at www.kyliedunn.com/toolkit.

www.ingramcontent.com/pod-product-compliance
Lightning Source LLC
Chambersburg PA
CBHW060426010526
44118CB00017B/2383